BE Z.O.E.

First Second Third **John**

Ages 5-7

Zealous Obedient Expectant

MaryBeth Clare

Be Z.O.E. Ages 5-7
is available at special quantity discounts for bulk purchase for sales promotions,
premiums, fund-raising, and educational needs.
For details write Endurance Press, 577 N Cardigan Ave, Star, ID 83669.

Visit Endurance Press' website at www.endurancepress.com

Be Z.O.E. Ages 5-7

PUBLISHED BY ENDURANCE PRESS
577 N Cardigan Ave
Star, ID 83669 U.S.A.

All rights reserved. Except for brief excerpts for review purposes,
no part of this book may be
reproduced or used in any form without
prior written permission from the publisher.

ISBN 978-0-998875675

®2019 MaryBeth Clare

Cover by Teal Rose Design Studios

Interior & Cover art by Darin Eason

Printed in the United States of America

First Edition 2019

Table of Contents

Introduction..Page 6-8

Week 1: Becoming God's Friend.............................Page 9-20
Overview of Genesis 1-3 and the Gospels

Week 2: Jesus is Alive and Forgives.........................Page 21-30
Matthew 28; Mark 16; Luke 24; 1st John 1

Week 3: God's Best Rules..Page 31-41
Matthew 22:37-39; Mark 12:30,31; Luke 10:27; 1st John 2

Week 4: House Rules..Page 42-52
Galatians 5:22-25; 1st John 3

Week 5: Outsmarting Satan Through Truth..............Page 53-62
Isaiah 14:12-17; Ezekiel 28:12-19; 1st John 4

Week 6: God's Promises are True............................Page 63-72
1st John 5

Week 7: Don't Believe Everything You Hear.............Page 73-82
John 10:22-42; Acts 1:9-11; 1st Corinthians 15:3-4; Second John

Week 8: Learning From The Good, The Bad, and The Ugly...
Third John   ...Page 83-93

Introduction

Welcome to Be Z.O.E.. Dr. James Strong paved the way for those of us who aren't Hebrew, Greek, or Aramaic scholars to study the Word in its original languages. In 1890, the first edition of Strong's Concordance was published. He gave us the definitions for every word in the original texts! These will be what I reference in our word studies. ***H*** is for Hebrew found mainly in the *Old Testament*. ***G*** is for Greek, and ***A*** is for Aramaic, these two are mainly in the *New Testament*. He used the King James translation (KJV). I encourage you to get out your Bible every time you open this study. You can read the passages in the translation you enjoy.

The Greek word for life is ZOE. There are three characteristics which are prudent to apply to our daily lives:

Z - *Zealous, G2207: To most eagerly desire.*

We need to desire our relationship with God on a daily basis. We can do this through prayer, journaling, being in the Word, fellowship, and the list goes on.

O - *Obedient, G5219: To listen, to submit.*

God has a plan and purpose for each person. When He created you, He thought of all the plans He had in store. We need to seek Him (through being Zealous) and ask Him what He requires of us daily. It could be a little thing or working on a dream you've had for many years. Within this we must be obedient to His calling, even when we might not understand. You will know His direction for your life as it lines up with the Word. He will not ask you to do something that ever goes against the Word.

E - *Expectant, H6960: To wait, to look for, to hope.*

One thing we are always to look for is our Messiah calling us home in the Rapture. He can come at any moment, and we are to be expectant. When we look to being expectant in daily life, God has many surprises for us throughout our lives. We need to be expectant of what He wants to do and look for the opportunities He brings to us.

Each section has seven sub-sections:

1. At the start of each week you'll have a Leader/Parent overview. This is here to help any parent/leader know what the key points are in the lesson.

2. We begin with a story format. Please read the Bible references listed under the lesson title before you begin. It is very important to be in the Bible at every age.

3. Next we take a deeper look. We will discuss some history, explain some words in their original language, and talk about how you can apply it to your daily life.

4. Seeing Z.O.E reflected. It's time to take an in-depth look at the lives of people from the Bible and how they show these three characteristics.

5. Here we have a memory verse and being Z.O.E.

6. Now it's time for some fun. Activity pages will reinforce the lesson all while having some fun.

7. We end with writing out a prayer to God. If you're learning how to write, ask an adult to help you.

Through all the studies we will talk a lot about salvation. There are three parts to salvation:

1. Justification: Jesus died, was buried, and rose again for your sins. Through this, your sins have been forgiven and you are justified.

2. Sanctification: The Holy Spirit wants to work in and through you. He will mold you into the image of Jesus. This process takes a lifetime. It is all about our growth in the Lord.

3. Glorification: This one will happen when we get to Heaven. We will have our glorified bodies. We will be permanently removed from the presence of sin!

You are a beautiful creation of God. He has a plan and purpose for you. By being in the Bible and learning how it applies to your life, you are delighting God. He is smiling over you. Before starting your study, please pray and ask the Holy Spirit to reveal truth to you.

It is my prayer that this will bring you closer to your Creator.

God's richest blessing and may He bring you much joy,

MaryBeth

Week 1

Becoming God's Friend

Leader/Parent Overview

The books of First, Second, and Third John are written to those who believe. Before we embark upon them it is vital for kids to understand sin and Jesus' free gift of salvation. This is the focus for this chapter.

Key points:

- Sin is disobedience to God and what He has commanded us.
- All humans sin.
- Sin separates God and humans.
- Jesus came to bring humans and God back together.
- Jesus is a part of God. You can explain that God is three parts. God the Father, God the Son, and God the Holy Spirit - The Trinity.
- Jesus loves you so much that He died, was buried, and lived again on the third day.
- Jesus' gift is free. We cannot do anything to earn it, and it is open to every person.
- Accepting His gift is asking Jesus into your heart. That means that you and God are no longer separated.
- The Holy Spirit comes and lives inside you, and helps you to live a life that makes God happy.

Some Additional Questions for discussion:

- What does it mean to disobey?
- What does it mean to love someone?
- How can you show someone you love them? How can you show Jesus you love Him?

Becoming God's Friend

An overview of Genesis 1-3 and the Gospels

Hello Friend,

My name is John, I lived thousands of years ago during the time of Jesus. Jesus had many followers, but there were twelve that went with Him when He traveled. I was one of them; a teenager as a matter of fact. Jesus became my friend and taught me a lot. I want to share some of His teachings with you. Jesus' teachings are just as important for you today as they were for us who lived long ago. I know that He wants you to learn what He taught. Mostly, He wants to be your friend.

Jesus is a part of the Triune God. Triune means there are three in one. There is God the Father, God the Son (who is Jesus), and God the Holy Spirit. All three work together as one. God was never created. He has always been. One day God decided to create man, the earth, the sky, and the universe. He created everything. God taught the first man and woman, Adam and Eve. He also gave them rules. He told them to not eat the fruit from a certain tree. Then a slithery creature came to Adam and Eve. He told them they would be like God if they would eat from the tree. One day Eve grabbed some fruit off the tree and bit into it. Adam also bit into the fruit. Oh how good it tasted for a second. Then they felt bad for disobeying God and hid.

That is how sin entered the world. When we disobey God we sin. Sin makes it to where we cannot be friends with God. Sin makes God sad. When God created everything He knew sin would come. He knew when He created you and me that we would sin.

Every person except Jesus has sinned. Before creating everything He came up with a plan so we could once again be His friend.

God asked many people to be a part of this plan and they said yes! One was Mary who was Jesus' mom. When Jesus grew up He went all around teaching about God. He taught us how to live a life which would make God happy. Jesus knew that His time of teaching would be short but would last forever. The best part of God's plan was about to take place.

There were some people who didn't like Jesus' teachings. They were evil in their heart and wanted Jesus to die. Jesus knew what they had planned because they were going to be a part of God's plan.

Jesus was arrested and went to court. He was found guilty even though He never did anything wrong. Jesus was told He would die on a cross.

As I heard these words I began to cry, I didn't want my friend to die. He had told us that He would die one day but I didn't think it would be when He was only 33 years old.

The Roman guards took Jesus and gave Him a very heavy cross. He and another man from the crowd carried it up the hill to the place where He would die. He was placed on the cross and the guards nailed Him there. They placed a nail in each of His hands and one in His feet. After the cross was lifted up, Jesus cried out saying "Father forgive them, they don't know what they are doing!" Before He died Jesus asked me to take care of His mom, Mary. When He died the sky became dark and there was a great earthquake. One of the Roman guards said "Surely He had to be God's Son." Hours later, the cross was taken down and His body was placed in a tomb. A tomb is like a cave. A stone was placed to cover the front.

The following days were Jewish holidays. There are rules for Jewish holidays, one is that we can't work. Jesus' body needed to be prepared for burial but that was considered work, so we waited. Three days passed and the holidays were over. One of Jesus' friends, Mary Magdalene, made it to the tomb before me. She saw that the tombstone was already rolled away. She went in wondering who was there. She found no one, not even Jesus' body! "Who could be so mean as to take His body?" she thought.

Now one of the twelve followers and I were not too far away. She ran to us and told us what happened. We all ran to it and I got there first. We remembered that Jesus said He would be raised from the dead. We all believed that is what happened. Jesus was alive again! Joyfully we went out to share the good news.

My friend, Jesus never disobeyed God. It is because of this, that when Jesus died He took the sins of the entire world on Him, including yours and mine.

Three days later He was alive again! This was God's plan so He could be friends with humans again. He asks that we believe in Jesus and what He did. This is called the gift of salvation. Do you accept His gift of friendship to you, His gift of salvation? If you do, He will help you to be obedient in your life and will be forgiving when you sin. He wants to be your friend and teach you through the Bible. If your answer is yes, the rest of this book will help you learn how to live a life that will make God smile. Please find an adult you trust who knows Jesus. Ask them questions. Ask them to pray with you. Praying is simply talking to God.

I hope that you've said yes to this friendship. He will be the best friend you will ever have. He will change your life just like He has changed mine.

Taking A Deeper Look

1. The Bible is filled with many great stories. All of these teach us something. What is your favorite Bible story? What did you learn?

_____
_____
_____
_____
_____

2. Do you see how much God loves you since Jesus died for you? Do you love God?

_____
_____
_____
_____
_____

3. This gift of salvation that Jesus has given you brings forgiveness for your sins. There is nothing you can do to pay God back for it. You don't have to do anything to earn it. It is like a present you get for your birthday. A person gives you the gift out of love for you. This is how it is with God. He loves you so much He wants to give you the gift of forgiveness. Do you accept His gift?

_____
_____
_____
_____
_____

Seeing Z.O.E. Reflected in this Passage

Z - God is *Zealous* for you and wants to be your friend. What does it mean to be a friend? How can you be God's friend?

_____
_____
_____
_____
_____

O - *Obedience* means you follow the rules. We have rules everywhere we go. They are at home, in school, at church. What are some rules you are good at *Obeying*?

_____
_____
_____
_____
_____

E - All of us sin and need to be forgiven. We can *Expect* that God will forgive us when we tell Him we are sorry. Have you told God you're sorry when you sin? How did you feel after you told Him and knew He forgave you?

_____
_____
_____
_____
_____

Memory Verse

"For I delivered to you as of first importance what I also received: that Christ died for our sins in accordance with the Scriptures, that he was buried, that he was raised on the third day in accordance with the Scriptures"
1st Corinthians 15:3-4

This verse gives us the Gospel in a few words. Why is it important that Jesus died, was buried, and lived again? Talk to an adult about this.

_____
_____
_____
_____
_____

Being Z.O.E.

This week we talked about obedience. God wants us to be obedient to our parents. Sometimes we are obedient by doing our chores. This week do your chores without being asked twice.

Which chores will you do without being asked?

_____
_____
_____
_____
_____

Becoming God's Friend

_____ is God's Friend.
      (YOUR NAME)

Becoming God's Friend

Directions: Match the numbers to the letters to reveal the answer

A	B	C	D	E	F	G	H	I	J	K	L	M
1	2	3	4	5	6	7	8	9	10	11	12	13

N	O	P	Q	R	S	T	U	V	W	X	Y	Z
14	15	16	17	18	19	20	21	22	23	24	25	26

Where Adam and Eve lived in the

__ __ __ __ __ __ __ __ __ __ __ __
7 1 18 4 5 14   15 6   5 4 5 14

God is __ __ __ __ __ __
       20 18 9 21 14 5

That means that He is three is one. All three work together as one. There is

God the __ __ __ __ __ __
         6 1 20 8 5 18

God the __ __ __ Whose name is __ __ __ __ __
        19 15 14   10 5 19 21 19

God the __ __ __ __   __ __ __ __ __ __
         8 15 12 25   19 16 9 18 9 20

When you ask Jesus into your heart You are

__ __ __ __ ' __ __ __ __ __ __ __
7 15 4 19   6   18 9 5 14 4

Becoming God's Friend

```
P R A C D P H V C J E X U A D
R A O U R X U R H L A A Z V E
T G N C J E U T J S J U B C V
H O G G H C A L E W G O U U E
T W M A W I F T M F S O H X G
K H R B H I H Z I U Q I Y N J
H G E J V F V L I O D H N Y K
H K Y E N A Z S D A N E R D R
D I O W I Z B J W E V E V N A
I X K I B E L I E V E K I P J
F X J S O F I K R X V V V N E
W S Z H J K A S Q O Y I H A X
W F F J D T X K T X W W J E Z
T H R E E O X L U L Z Q N A A
A D A M A S T I E H H S E U H
```

ADAM	BELIEVE	CREATION
EVE	JEWISH	JOHN
SIN	THREE	TOMB

Dear God,

Your Friend,

Week 2

Jesus is Alive and God Forgives!

Leader/Parent Overview

Key Points:

- Jesus was a human just like you and me. He felt all the emotions we feel, had a family, and grew up. One of the big differences is that He lived a perfect life. He never sinned. It is because of this that He was able to bring God and humans back together.

- Once we accept Jesus' free gift of salvation we no longer choose or have a desire to sin. We will sin but it is not something that we will make a habit of doing. Instead we want to tell the truth and live according to God's commandments.

- John tells us that once we accept Jesus' free gift we are in fellowship with God. This means that we are partners (literally in the Greek) with God. Some kids might better understand this being described as friendship. He does things for us and we do things for Him.

Some Additional Questions

- What is a lie? What is truth? What is the difference between truths and lies?

- What is a habit? How can you make telling the truth a habit?

- What are some things God has done for you? What are some things you have done for God?

- How can you be God's partner/friend?

Jesus is Alive and God Forgives!

Matthew 28; Mark 16; Luke 24; John 20,21; 1st John 1

Hello Friend, Where did I leave off? That's right, when three of us found the empty tomb.

After finding the tomb empty and believing that Jesus was alive again, Jesus came to us. First, Jesus visited Mary Magdalene, our friend that got to the tomb before us. Later, He came and visited some of the twelve followers, including me! At another time, Cleopas and another person went walking from Jerusalem to Emmaus. That is a seven mile walk! Somewhere along the way Jesus met them and spoke with them for a while. One day, early in the morning, He came to the sea. He saw that we were fishing there. We caught some fish and then we all had breakfast. This was a fun way to start our day.

Over 500 people saw Him. They heard His voice and touched Him. Some of these people believed that He was God's Son, Jesus. They believed the Truth. They believed that He died for our sins, was buried, then He lived again! Jesus was able to do this because He is God's Son. After appearing to many people, Jesus decided it was time go to back home. Jesus did not die a second time but instead God the Father brought Him back into Heaven. Jesus is now in Heaven praying for you and me.

In Heaven there are no lights, no lamps, no light bulbs. There isn't even a sun or moon. But it is not dark at night there either. This is because God is light and He makes all of Heaven bright!

Do you want to know something else God is? He is forgiving! When we are disobedient, we sin. This makes us dirty inside. All we need to do is tell Him we are sorry. Then He will forgive us and make us clean again. He does this because of what Jesus has done for us.

Taking a Deeper Look

1. What do you think it means when you're told "God is light"? What do you imagine Him to look like?

_____
_____
_____
_____

2. Jesus was human, like you and me. Whenever you go through a hard time or a joyful time, tell Jesus about it. Since He was human and lived on Earth He can understand what you're going through. Share a hard or joyful time you've gone through.

_____
_____
_____
_____

3. We all have to clean our bodies. We wash behind our ears and wear clean clothes. Many times we don't think of how we look on the inside. Sin makes us dirty. When we don't tell God what we have done and repent, which means to apologize, the dirt can build up. It could get so dirty that it looks like a mud puddle! As often as we clean up on the outside we should clean up on the inside.

God sees your inside all the time. How much sin (dirt) do you think He sees? Why should you be clean on the inside too?

_____
_____
_____
_____

Seeing Z.O.E. Reflected in this Passage

Z - Since God is *Zealous* for you, He is able to make right something you have done wrong. He does this through forgiving. Someone might do something that hurts your feelings. You can show that person that you love God by forgiving them. Has someone hurt your feelings? Have you forgiven them even if they did not say they were sorry?

_____
_____
_____
_____
_____

O - We all sin and disobey God, even grownups. In *Obedience* we need to tell God what we have done wrong and ask for forgiveness. What are some things you have done wrong? Have you asked God for forgiveness?

_____
_____
_____
_____
_____

E - You can *Expect* that God will always love you. How do you show your love to God?

_____
_____
_____
_____
_____

Memory Verse

"For you, O Lord, are good and forgiving, abounding in steadfast love to all who call upon you."

Psalm 86:5

God has oodles of love and kindness. One way He gives them to us is through forgiveness. How do you show love, kindness, and forgiveness to others?

_____
_____
_____
_____
_____

Being Z.O.E.

This week if you hurt someone's feelings, be quick to tell them you're sorry. If someone hurts your feelings, be quick to forgive. What did you learn by doing this?

_____
_____
_____
_____
_____

Jesus Is Alive!

Draw what you think he looks like!

Jesus is Alive and Forgives

Directions: Match the numbers to the letters to reveal the answer

A	B	C	D	E	F	G	H	I	J	K	L	M
1	2	3	4	5	6	7	8	9	10	11	12	13
N	O	P	Q	R	S	T	U	V	W	X	Y	Z
14	15	16	17	18	19	20	21	22	23	24	25	26

The Road From Jerusalem to Emmaus is

___ ___ ___ ___ ___   ___ ___ ___ ___ ___
19   5   22 5   14   13   9   12 5   19

Right now Jesus is in

___ ___ ___ ___ ___ ___
8   5   1   22 5   14

Jesus is ___ ___ ___ ___ ___ ___ ___ for us
         16 18 1   25 9   14 7

Heaven is bright because God is ___ ___ ___ ___ ___
                                 12 9   7   8   20

We need to tell God we are sorry when we sin. When we do this we

___ ___ ___ ___ ___ ___
18 5   16 5   14 20

Jesus is Alive and Forgives

```
F Y M R E P E N T P S Q H M W
K Y A U N I Y C K Z U Z A B X
Z P A P A M O K B K Y W O Y W
D Y Q P P K C F M G D G S R I
M F M P W E A T I H Z O L Q T
O M F R E N A G T S O H I T N
G E N S P D S R Y Z H U D O E
F O F B P C Y S I H E E I O S
S L I U L D V U J N X C R B S
I Q M W O G E P Y M G K T E N
D S U R V A B H J Y D Y Y M K
A D A O E U K B R I G H T A E
R M B E Z L U A H L A F U Y C
L J S B K K N Z E J V D Q V C
B I L I G H T C L E A N M T J
```

APPEARING   BRIGHT   CLEAN

DIRTY   FISH   LIGHT

LOVE   REPENT   WITNESS

Dear God,

Your Friend,

Week 3

God's Best Rules

Leader/Parent Overview

Key Points:

- Understand the difference between Advocate and Propitiation. Often these words are thought to be synonymous but they're not.
- An Advocate is a person. It is one who comes to one's aid.
- Propitiation is usually a verb. It is an action that is done in order to appease/stop the wrath of another.
- In our case Jesus is our Advocate. Through His completed work on the cross, He brought propitiation. He appeased the wrath of God through His sacrifice.
- Explain God's two greatest commandments: Love God with all your heart, mind, soul, and strength. Second, to love your neighbor as yourself.
- We can look to Jesus as our example in living these out perfectly.

Additional Questions

- How did Jesus love God with all of Himself?
- How did Jesus show love to you?
- How does the Holy Spirit help you to love others?
- What are some kind, loving actions we can express toward others?

God's Best Rules

Matthew 22:37-39; Mark 12:30,31; Luke 10:27; 1st John 2

Hello Friend,

The day my best friend Jesus died I was sad. Then three days later when He lived again, I was very happy! What Jesus did was part of God's plan. God wanted to show the world how much He loves every person. He wanted everyone to know that they could be part of His family. God sent Jesus to die for the sins of the world. The forgiveness that God gives comes from believing in Jesus and what He did. Jesus died a very painful death, was buried, resurrected, and ascended back into Heaven.

One day Jesus was asked what the two best commandments are. Commandments are rules we live by. He said the first is to love God with all of you. Which means you love God from the top of your head to the tips of your toes. The second is to love each other. We can love others because God loves us.

Do you know what makes these two rules even better? We have a living, breathing example. This person lived without ever sinning once. What are your guesses? Yes it's Jesus! The first four books of the New Testament tell us how Jesus lived.

When you believe in Jesus, God gives you a helper. This Helper is the Holy Spirit. He comes and lives inside you. He will help you love people. He will help you understand the Bible. He will tell you when you sin and He helps you to not sin as much. He will help you live a life that makes God happy! Anything you need help with just ask the Holy Spirit.

There are so many great gifts God gives you when you accept Jesus. Another one is everlasting life. When a Christian dies they will go to Heaven and live with Jesus forever.

Taking a Deeper Look

1. The Holy Spirit is our Helper. What do you need help with? Ask the Holy Spirit and He will help you.

_____
_____
_____
_____
_____

2. We are to love God with all of our being. How do you show God you love Him from the top of your head to your tippy toes?

_____
_____
_____
_____
_____

3. One day all the people who have accepted Jesus will be in Heaven. What do you think it will be like to spend every day with Jesus?

_____
_____
_____
_____
_____

Seeing Z.O.E. Reflected in this Passage

Z - Show God and others that you are *Zealous* to follow His rules. Do this through showing love to others. What are some things you can do to show others God's love?

_____
_____
_____
_____
_____

O - Jesus told us the two best rules: Love God with all of you and love others. Love is a choice and not just a good feeling. How *Obedient* are you in loving God and people?

_____
_____
_____
_____
_____

E - Everyone who believes in Jesus and what He did for us can *Expect* to go to Heaven when they die. What do you think Jesus will look like? Do you have any questions for Him?

_____
_____
_____
_____
_____

Memory Verse

"For God so loved the world, that he gave his only Son, that whoever believes in him should not perish but have eternal life."

John 3:16

God gave the world a gift of salvation through Jesus. Part of this gift is everlasting life. There are some who do not accept it and there are some who do. Every person has to make their own choice.

Why do you think it is important to God that everyone make their own choice?

_____
_____
_____
_____
_____

How big do you think God's love for you is? Mark it on the line below:

_____

NOT VERY MUCH   **MORE THAN I COULD EVER KNOW**

Being Z.O.E.

God loves you so very, very much Friend. He loves you so much that He wants to talk with you. You can do this by praying and reading the Bible. Every day this week make sure you pray and read or listen to the Bible.

Week Day	Did I pray?		Did I read or listen to the Bible?	
Sunday	Yes	No	Yes	No
Monday	Yes	No	Yes	No
Tuesday	Yes	No	Yes	No
Wednesday	Yes	No	Yes	No
Thursday	Yes	No	Yes	No
Friday	Yes	No	Yes	No
Saturday	Yes	No	Yes	No

God's Best Rules

Love God From The Top of your Head to your Tippy Toes

God's Best Rules

Directions: Match the numbers to the letters to reveal the answer

A	B	C	D	E	F	G	H	I	J	K	L	M
1	2	3	4	5	6	7	8	9	10	11	12	13

N	O	P	Q	R	S	T	U	V	W	X	Y	Z
14	15	16	17	18	19	20	21	22	23	24	25	26

God's first best rule tells us we are to

__ __ __ __   __ __ __
12 15 22 5   7 15 4

With __ __ __ of __ __
      1 12 12   13 5

God's second best rule is to

__ __ __ __   __ __ __ __
12 15 22 5   5 1 3 8

__ __ __ __ __
15 20 8 5 18

God's Best Rules

```
H J O S E K Y J O N W D R P S
G A K R T K V B T N T Y B B O
H H R W W R F Q P U A Z J R H
I E Q D X H E V K M L W K P H
B D R H G E X N J L Q D I L R
G E T E A A T D G B V D M A D
U Q S D Z R X X G T A S I N S
X Q D T R T G F F B H A N B O
N A V F M Y Z Z O A A E D T U
U H Y L W J L V H D M D E F L
G I F T S M K O I X G I L A I
L G U A K F Q G R W G T L D J
J D I Q Y J L Q J Y X E Q Y S
A Y T Y G U L Z C E Z R K N O
J R U L E S O N I Y A T I F I
```

BEST   FAMILY   GIFTS

HEART   MIND   PLAN

RULES   SOUL   STRENGTH

Dear God,

Your Friend,

Week 4

House Rules

Leader/Parent Overview

Key Points

- This week spend a lot of time talking about God's immense love for each person. If you can, tell each child individually that God loves him/her.

- In this chapter John speaks again on how a child of God doesn't sin. Remind the kids that we will sin but we don't do it on purpose or make a habit of it.

- Moreover, when we do sin God is ready and willing to forgive. A favorite example of mine is how we must clean our skin when it gets dirty. It is like that with sin. We get dirty on the inside from it and it needs to be cleaned. Tell God you are sorry and ask Him to help you work on not sinning. He is always ready to forgive!

Additional Questions

- Why do you think John wants to remind us that God's kids don't make a habit of lying?

- How does knowing God loves you change the way you behave?

- Do you think that you should act differently being God's kid?

House Rules

Galatians 5:22-25; 1st John 3

Hello Friend,

God loves you so much. The whole world and the universe couldn't contain the amount of love He has for you. You are His kid and He is your Heavenly Father.

All of us have friends and family. We want to tell them about our day and what is going on in our lives. Guess what? God wants that too! He wants you to tell Him all your dreams, what's happening in your day, your problems, and what you've done well. He wants to hear you tell Him all of it! God wants to be a part of your daily life. He will always answer you. Sometimes He tells us "yes", other times "no", and many times "maybe, just wait." Friend, God wants what is best for you. Sometimes what we want and think is best doesn't match up with what God knows is best. The more you get to know Him, the more your desires will line up with what He wants for you.

Do you remember our talk about the Holy Spirit? God gives us Him as our Helper. He helps us to not sin as much. He takes us through a life long journey on becoming more like Jesus. He helps us to know when we have disobeyed and reminds us we need to ask for forgiveness. When we tell God we are sorry He forgives our sins.

He also will help teach us how to behave. What we say should line up with how we act. For instance if you say you love God then your actions should show it. As God's kid your actions should show love, kindness, goodness, peace, faithfulness, self-control, patience, gentleness, and joy. These are the Fruit of the Spirit. These are actions that show people God is working in you.

Taking a Deeper Look

1. What is prayer? How often do you pray?

_____
_____
_____
_____
_____

2. What prayers has God answered?

_____
_____
_____
_____
_____

3. Christians are God's kids. How we behave and act around others matters. What are some actions that show good and nice behavior?

_____
_____
_____
_____
_____

Seeing Z.O.E. Reflected in this Passage

Z - God shows He is *Zealous* for you through His actions. One way to show others you love God is through your actions. Let's look at three actions you can do today.

How can you:

Be Kind _____

Be Helpful _____

Be Forgiving _____

O - The Holy Spirit helps us to be more *Obedient*. He also helps us become more like Jesus. Jesus was always *Obedient* and is our greatest example. Jesus is loving, even to people who don't like Him. He is kind and forgiving.

What are some other things Jesus is? What Jesus-like actions are you good at doing? Which ones need work?

_____

_____

_____

_____

_____

E - No matter what, the Holy Spirit will always be with you when you are God's kid. Even when you sin or are naughty you can *Expect* the Holy Spirit to be with you. He is a part of God. There is God the Father, Jesus the Son, and the Holy Spirit. He will never leave you. You can rest and *Expect* Him to help you. How does that truth make you feel?

_____

_____

_____

_____

_____

Memory Verse

"So you shall keep my commandments and do them: I am the Lord."
Leviticus 22:31

There are many commandments, or rules, which God has given us. You can find all of them in the Bible. One of them tells us we are to honor our mom and dad. This means we are to value/respect them. Even grown-ups need to value/respect their parents.

What can you do to show your mom and dad that you love and value/respect them?

_____
_____
_____
_____
_____

Being Z.O.E.

The way a Christian acts matters. As we've talked about, we need to show love, goodness, and kindness. Everyday this week find someone you can extend one of these things to. You could draw a picture for them, give them a hug, forgive someone if they've hurt you. There are many ways you can do this.

Write down what you did and have learned:

_____
_____
_____
_____
_____

House Rules

LOVE, JOY, KINDNESS, GOODNESS, PEACE, PATIENCE, FAITHFULNESS, SELF-CONTROL, GENTLENESS

_____ has the Fruit of the Spirit.
(YOUR NAME)

House Rules

Draw a picture of you living out the Fruit of the Spirit
(For example: You could be doing a chore or helping someone)

House Rules

Directions: Match the numbers to the letters to reveal the answer

A	B	C	D	E	F	G	H	I	J	K	L	M
1	2	3	4	5	6	7	8	9	10	11	12	13

N	O	P	Q	R	S	T	U	V	W	X	Y	Z
14	15	16	17	18	19	20	21	22	23	24	25	26

The Fruit of the Spirit are

___ ___ ___ ___   ___ ___ ___
12 15 22 5   10 15 25

___ ___ ___ ___ ___ ___ ___ ___
11 9   14 4   14 5   19 19

___ ___ ___ ___ ___ ___ ___ ___
7   15 15 4   14 5   19 19

___ ___ ___ ___ ___
16 5   1   3   5

___ ___ ___ ___ ___ ___ ___ ___ ___ ___ ___ ___
6   1   9   20 8   6   21 12 14 5   19 19

___ ___ ___ ___ - ___ ___ ___ ___ ___ ___ ___
19 5   12 6   3   15 14 20 18 15 12

___ ___ ___ ___ ___ ___ ___ ___
16 1   20 9   5   14 3   5

___ ___ ___ ___ ___ ___ ___ ___ ___ ___
7   5   14 20 12 5   14 5   19 19

House Rules

```
O I Q R O H G T M E Y U S O U Z C A A G
F R A S M L U U A I W O K D C H C X V W
L N F E P P Y A H X C V V J M H G O K O
M J A L T Y K Z V U F Q B A E L O V E C
H N I F H A X I W L Y P V G F J Q M Z A
H P T C R S O D N K G Z X X G P U N P M
P V H O Q P G C U D W P P B O E Y U B H
Y W F N O I M D W H N A G N O F A J G C
V H U T M R D C J H K E K Z D H M J L T
V X L R G I C X A I S K S D N L P B L Y
S Q N O I T D I I Q F A V S E K F U T M
B H E L R Q Y J I I I M V A S M X E C C
Z I S E L Q B S M T C G W K S R S P W K
O Q S N T F T Z A V U G I A Y N W Q K G
N L Q Y O H X V Z U W W U J A V J M W F
C M B J J R U L O R D B F D T M G J O R
Q R A A X S H O Z G R N A O R Z T K Y U
N P A T I E N C E L S B X O G Q Y B F I
C Q U U K K G S J I T C P K S X B B H T
G K Z K W B X D F C P L P E A C E F L B
```

FAITHFULNESS	FRUIT	GOODNESS
KINDNESS	LOVE	PATIENCE
PEACE	SELFCONTROL	SPIRIT

Dear God,

Your Friend,

Week 5

Outsmarting Satan Through Truth

Leader/Parent Overview

- I suggest that you read 2nd Peter 2 and Jude in preparation for this study. This week John tells us that every believer will have times of testing in their lives. Part of passing the test is knowing the Bible. In the above passages we are given several characteristics of false teachers. Perhaps you can write down a few that stand out to you and you can share and discuss them with the kids, ie. they deny that Jesus is Lord.

- There are two main truths we need to continually reinforce: (1) The Gospel is that Jesus died, was buried, and rose again. (2) Jesus is the only way to Heaven.

- Express to them the importance of daily listening to or reading the Bible. Even if it's only a couple of minutes a day, the Word goes into the heart and stays. In times of difficulty and testing the Holy Spirit will bring Scripture back to our memory.

Some Additional Questions

- What are some characteristics God's kids should have? Some examples would be the love, joy, kindness, servant's heart, etc.
- How much time do you spend reading or listening to the Bible?

Outsmarting Satan Through Truth

Isaiah 14:12-17; Ezekiel 28:12-19; 1st John 4

Hello Friend,

A very, very long time ago God created angels. The Number One angel was very beautiful. One day this angel decided he wanted to be God. He was filled with jealousy and pride. There was one BIG problem, he was created and something that is created can never become better than the Creator. This angel's name is Satan. Due to his disobedience, jealously, and pride God kicked him out of Heaven. He and one third of the angels fell all the way to Earth. He is God's enemy. He doesn't want people to know the Truth about God.

Satan is very sneaky and tricky. He was in the garden of Eden. Now he roams around the Earth. Satan is very smart but he doesn't know everything. He doesn't know what you're thinking. He does know if you believe in Jesus and have accepted His gift of salvation. Now that you're God's kid, he is going to try to trick you. In his tricking, he is deceiving. There is good news. You have the Holy Spirit. The Holy Spirit will give you the smarts to win when Satan tries his tricks! You can win because of the Holy Spirit and because of Jesus' work. You are on the winning side. Whenever you feel like Satan is trying to trick you, tell him that you're not going to fall for it. No Siree! You tell him the Truth and that you're on the side that has already won. Then pray and tell God what happened. Thank Him that you won and ask Him to keep on helping you. Satan can get very tricky and we need God to give us the smarts to know when it is happening. One way to get those smarts is to read the Bible.

When I lived in Ephesus, there were many people who taught wrong about Jesus. Let me tell you what is true. Your faith and belief in Jesus and all He did rests on these facts: He lived a sinless life, He died, He was buried, and He lives again! If anyone tries to teach you anything different, be careful. They might be trying to trick you into believing in something false. If you ever are unsure, pray and ask God for help. You can also talk to an adult you trust who knows Jesus.

One thing that sets Christians apart is their love. Remember to love God from the top of your head to your tippy toes. You can do this by following His rules. Since God loves you, you can love others. God's love is perfect.

Taking A Deeper Look

1. God is real and filled with love. Why do you think Satan does not want people knowing the Truth about God?

_____
_____
_____
_____
_____

2. Satan is filled with jealousy and pride. What are jealousy and pride? If you don't know find an adult and ask them.

_____
_____
_____
_____
_____

3. John tells us that God's love is perfect. Describe perfect love.

_____
_____
_____
_____
_____

Seeing Z.O.E. Reflected in this Passage

Z - God is *Zealous* for you and knows that Satan would be sneaky and tricky. He has given us the Holy Spirit and the Bible. He gives us everything we need to outsmart Satan. Has Satan been sneaky and tricky to you? What happened?

_____
_____
_____
_____
_____

O - Being jealous and prideful are ways in which we can be *Disobedient*. To be jealous means that you don't like someone because of something good they've done and you want the attention they are getting. To be prideful means that you think you are better than other people. The opposite of these are being friendly, loving, and humble. When you are friendly, loving, and humble you are being *Obedient*. How can you be friendly, loving, and humble?

_____
_____
_____
_____
_____

E - You are God's kid. You can *Expect* that God's enemy Satan will try to trick you. One of the best ways to not be tricked is to read or listen to the Bible.

How often do you read or listen to the Bible? What is your favorite Bible verse?

_____
_____
_____
_____
_____

Memory Verse

"But thanks be to God, who gives us the victory through our Lord Jesus Christ."

1st Corinthians 15:57

There is victory in Jesus! Victory over sin. Victory over being tricked/deceived by Satan. These victories are given to you because of what Jesus has done! Write out a note of praise to God for this gift.

_____
_____
_____
_____
_____

Being Z.O.E.

This week when you start to feel prideful or jealous or bratty ask God to help you. Take a few moments and ask Him to change that in you. It won't be easy but the Holy Spirit can do it. Remember the victory that Jesus has given you! You can be victorious here! Write about your week:

_____
_____
_____
_____
_____

Outsmarting Satan Through Truth

The Bible is God's Word and Truth

_____ Believes and reads the Bible
(YOUR NAME)

My Bible

My Favorite Bible Verse is
_____
_____
_____
_____

Outsmarting Satan Through Truth

Directions: Match the numbers to the letters to reveal the answer

A	B	C	D	E	F	G	H	I	J	K	L	M
1	2	3	4	5	6	7	8	9	10	11	12	13
N	O	P	Q	R	S	T	U	V	W	X	Y	Z
14	15	16	17	18	19	20	21	22	23	24	25	26

What did God create a very, very long time ago

____ ____ ____ ____ ____ ____
 1   14   7   5   12   19

What was the name of the number 1 angel, who was very beautiful

____ ____ ____ ____ ____
 19   1   20   1   14

Satan doesn't want you to know the ____ ____ ____ ____ ____
                                                                 20   18   21   20   8

about ____ ____ ____
         7   15   4

The ____ ____ ____ ____   ____ ____ ____ ____ ____ ____
       8   15   12   25   19   16   9   18   9   20

and the ____ ____ ____ ____ ____ help you to know the truth
           2   9   2   12   5

about God

Outsmarting Satan Through Truth

```
V T A H R X C W H X M H S W I
I S R E V M M H H Q Q Y B X R
C F O U T J S H P U C S I Q V
T F H E S J U A Y Z Y F B N Q
O W D L T T H J T T A X L H T
R J E K B J T F N A V Z E Q X
Y E U L A X D P A F N X I O T
L I M A N G E L S T T C P J R
S P N P P P G R U M J R S H I
Q M I X E Q L G X U Y E U L C
S V H A Z H A I O G I A P P K
Y P Z J M Z F E G D E T H U I
R B I P C V W R Y I M O N D N
G H O L Y N Y A C C X R G B G
D Z D E A Z W Q Q G S C M J K
```

ANGELS	BIBLE	CREATOR
GOD	HOLY	SATAN
TRICKING	TRUST	VICTORY

Dear God,

Your Friend,

Week 6

God's Promises Are True

Leader/Parent Overview

Key Points

- We will be looking at eight assurances of our salvation. It would be good to go over the tenses of salvation with the kids.

- First, we are justified, this happens right when we say yes to Jesus' free gift. We are then sealed with the Holy Spirit. This happens once.

- Secondly, we are sanctified. This is a life long process of being molded into the image of Jesus. As Christians we are to help each other along in our walks. Encourage the kids to help one another in their walks.

- Lastly, we are glorified. This will happen in our future. We no longer will have these human bodies but will have glorified ones.

Additional Questions

- It would be fun to brainstorm with the kids on ways they could help each other in their walks. Maybe they could read the Bible together, help each other memorize Scripture, etc. If you have time, get a poster board and write all their ideas on it. This would be a very fun activity.

God's Promises Are True

1st John 5

Hello Friend,

This is the last part of my first letter. I often say the same thing over and over. This is because I want to make sure you understand. There are eight truths you need to know.

1. God is love. When you believe and accept Jesus' free gift of salvation you become a part of God's family. He asks that His children obey His rules. We show others that we belong to God by following His rules.

2. We are on the winning side of the battle between God and Satan. Anytime Satan tries to trick you or lie to you, you don't need to worry. You are on the winning side. God has given you the Holy Spirit to help you.

3. Jesus is God. When Jesus lived on Earth, He was all-God and all-man. The first step in winning these battles is saying and believing that Jesus is the Son of God who takes away sin!

4. Since you're God's kid you will be spending your everlasting life with Jesus!

5. God answers your prayers.

6. Even though you still sin, you don't purposefully go and sin. You want to live life according to God's rules.

7. Sin and evil should bother Christians. These are things that God doesn't like and are things we need to avoid.

8. God is real, God is true. We serve a living God! This separates us from all other religions.

My last word of advice in this letter is to not like idols. An idol is anyone or anything that you place above God. Idols can cause a lot of trouble in your life. Idols are something Satan uses when he is being sneaky and tricky. It is never too early to learn that! Remember God's number one rule: Love God with all of you.

Taking a Deeper Look

1. Which one of the truths do you like the best? Why?

_____
_____
_____
_____
_____

2. What is the difference between accidentally sinning and purposefully sinning?

_____
_____
_____
_____
_____

3. An idol is something that takes God's number 1 spot in our lives. It doesn't matter what age someone is, we all need to ask the Holy Spirit if we have an idol in our lives. Take a few moments and ask Him. If you do, tell God you are sorry and ask Him to remove it. Tell God you want Him to be number 1 again. Write out anything you want to remember about your prayer time.

_____
_____
_____
_____
_____

Seeing Z.O.E. Reflected in this Passage

Z - God is *Zealous* to have you in His family. Do you Desire (*Zealous*) to be in His family? What does it mean to you to be God's kid?

_____
_____
_____
_____
_____

O - Following God's rules should be something that makes us happy! When we do this we are being *Obedient* to God. Write down three of God's rules.

_____
_____
_____
_____
_____

E - You can *Expect* God to answer your prayers. It may not be the answer you want but He will answer it according to what is best for you. What are some things you've prayed for?

_____
_____
_____
_____
_____

Memory Verse

"For the wages of sin is death, but the free gift of God is eternal life in Christ Jesus our Lord."

Romans 6:23

Before you accepted Jesus' gift of salvation you were stuck in sin. You couldn't get free from it no matter what you did. Jesus set you free then gave you life.

What does it mean to you to be set free from sin? What are you looking most forward to in Heaven with Jesus?

_____
_____
_____
_____
_____

Being Z.O.E

There is so much more to our faith in God than simply believing. Accepting Jesus' gift and believing are the first steps in our new life. God wants us to show the world how much He loves them. He will use you in many ways to do this. He might have you tell someone about Jesus. He could ask you to extend love to a mean person. The list is never ending. Every day you should be ready to share God's love with people. Everyday this week ask yourself if you're ready. If you're not and feel nervous ask the Holy Spirit to help you. When God called Moses to help Him free the Israelites from Egypt, Moses was nervous too! Are you ready to put your faith in action?

_____
_____
_____
_____
_____

God's Promises Are True

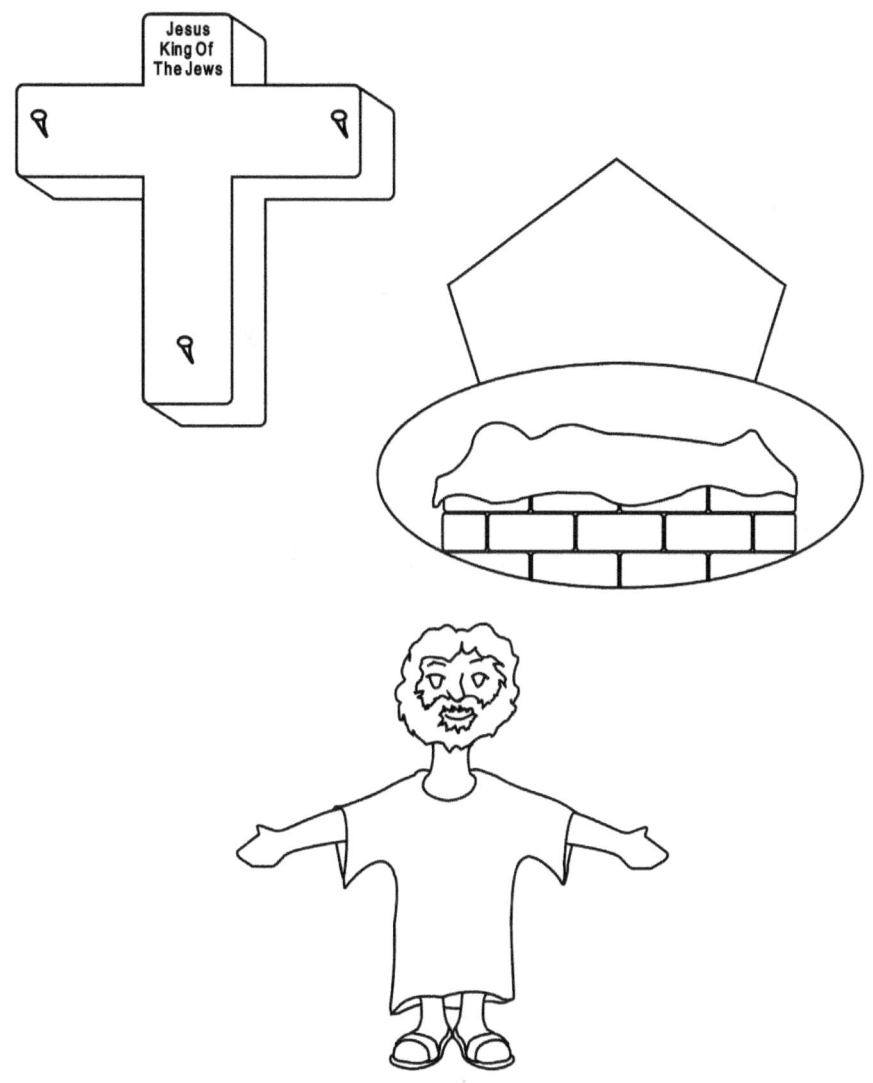

God's Promises Are True

Directions: Match the numbers to the letters to reveal the answer

A	B	C	D	E	F	G	H	I	J	K	L	M
1	2	3	4	5	6	7	8	9	10	11	12	13

N	O	P	Q	R	S	T	U	V	W	X	Y	Z
14	15	16	17	18	19	20	21	22	23	24	25	26

___ ___ ___ is ___ ___ ___ ___
7   15   4   12   15   22   5

God has ___ ___ ___ the ___ ___ ___ ___ ___
        23   15   14   2   1   20   20   12   5

___ ___ ___ ___ ___ is ___ ___ ___
10   5   19   21   19   7   15   4

Every one who accepts Jesus free gift of salvation becomes God's kid. All His kids get

___ ___ ___ ___ ___ ___ ___ ___ ___ ___ life
5   22   5   18   12   1   19   20   9   14   7

God ___ ___ ___ ___ ___ ___ ___ prayer
     1   14   19   23   5   18   19

Live life according to God's ___ ___ ___ ___ ___
                               18   21   12   5   19

___ ___ ___ and ___ ___ ___ ___ should bother Christians
19   9   14   5   22   9   12

God is ___ ___ ___ ___ and God is ___ ___ ___ ___
       18   5   1   12   20   18   21   5

God's Promises Are True

```
Q G P J E K D U P G K D M Z O
B X A R E F R I F L O W M D D
Z R D N O U K E I U I S S A M
F S E F S M R B T H C F U F A
G D Q Z I W I W U G I F E J Z
H G W P L M E S C Q J R O H D
Q J C C P W P R E A I B B J E
C F R V B U D P S F F K M G N
F B Z N L H R W S M Z C A G G
P R A Y E R W H M F P S N N O
D W Y D N B P W R G H O C F D
E V E R L A S T I N G U E T U
V L H V C D I H A Q B L G U S
E N A C T B V U O X Y F V L M
H U P A W S A L V A T I O N O
```

ANSWERS   EVERLASTING   GOD

LIFE   MAN   PRAYER

PROMISE   SALVATION   SOUL

Dear God,

Your Friend,

Week 7

Don't Believe Everything You Hear

Leader/Parent Overview

Key Points

- This lesson falls in line with the one on 1st John 4. It would be good to review the lessons on being tested and characteristics of false teachers.

- Ask the kids who they think the most important woman in history is and why. You can give them these clues: She lived during Jesus' time, she has a sister, she had children, she is loved by all who believe in Jesus. The answer we're looking for is Mary Jesus' mother.

- One point to emphasize is that John is reminding her of God's two greatest commandments. Even Jesus' mom needs reminding!

- Since we are partners with God we should tell others about God and encourage them to believe in Jesus. Work with the kids on how to share the Gospel: Jesus died, was buried, and lived again. Through this He conquered sin and death! When you accept His gift you too can be given everlasting life, be forgiven of sin, and live a life that makes God happy.

Additional Questions

- In place of additional questions, I highly encourage you to have the kids practice sharing the Gospel with each other. You're never too young to learn!

Don't Believe Everything You Hear

John 10:22-42; Acts 1:9-11; 1st Corinthians 15:3-4; Second John

Hello Friend,

This letter is to the most important woman in all of history, her children, and the church. How I loved walking with Jesus and learning from Him. He is our greatest example in loving God and loving others. Although we will never be perfect we must follow His lead and love. I encourage you to love God with all of you. From the moment you get up, until your bed time, and all through the night tell God you love Him.

I regret not being able to be with you in Ephesus. Even though I am not with you I have heard about those who don't believe in Jesus are coming to your homes. Being your Pastor I want to share wisdom with you in dealing with these people. Be sure that you do not listen to their teachings. Some of them teach that Jesus wasn't God's son. Others say He didn't rise from the dead. They are false teachers and bring confusion. If you listen to what they say you might start questioning your faith. These people are being used by Satan, God's enemy to trick and lie to you. Please be careful.

The truth is Jesus is God's son. He lived a perfect life, died, was buried, resurrected, and ascended into Heaven. When you believe in Jesus and accept His gift you have a new birth. This one is spiritual, one that happens inside you. You are also given the Holy Spirit. Your new birth sets you apart from people who don't believe. If you have friends who don't know Jesus or believe in Him, tell them about Him! If you happen to meet someone who doesn't know Jesus and is mean when you tell them about your faith, do not become friends with them. They could cause you a lot of trouble. Our world is filled with many who become angry and mean about Jesus. You will meet them when you're growing up, in college, and when you're an adult. They just never go away. Even though they are not your friends, it is good to pray for them. God loves them even though they don't love Him.

Taking a Deeper Look

1. Have you met someone who was mean when you spoke about Jesus? What happened? If not, what would you say?

_____
_____
_____
_____
_____

2. It is important that you know the truth about Jesus. When someone tries to tell you something false about Him you can tell them the truth.

What is the truth about Jesus? Hint, we talked about it a lot in 1st John.

_____
_____
_____
_____
_____

3. What are some lies that you have heard about Jesus? When you hear them are you able to speak the truth?

_____
_____
_____
_____
_____

Seeing Z.O.E. Reflected in this Passage

Z - In all of our lives, somebody has told us about Jesus. How He *Zealously* (Desires) wants us to know of His gift of salvation. Who told you about Jesus? Have you told anyone about Jesus?

_____
_____
_____
_____
_____

O - Christians should be friends with other Christians. Together you can talk about God, what Jesus has done for you, and what the Holy Spirit is doing in your life. How have you been *Obedient* in this?

_____
_____
_____
_____
_____

E - We can *Expect* to be challenged in our love for others at times. Love is not always easy. It is something we choose to do. God *Expects* His kids, young ones and old ones alike, to be loving. Have you been challenged in loving? What happened?

_____
_____
_____
_____
_____

Memory Verse

"Love is patient and kind; love does not envy or boast; it is not arrogant"
1st Corinthians 13:4

What does it mean to be kind and patient?

_____
_____
_____

What does it mean to have envy, to boast, or be proud?

_____
_____
_____
_____

What are kind things you can do?

_____
_____
_____
_____

Being Z.O.E.

Show kindness this week. Use some of the examples of kindness you listed. What did you do? Did you make those you were kind to happy?

_____
_____
_____

Don't Believe Everything You Hear

_____ Can tell others about Jesus.
(YOUR NAME)

Don't Believe Everything You Hear

Directions: Match the numbers to the letters to reveal the answer

A	B	C	D	E	F	G	H	I	J	K	L	M
1	2	3	4	5	6	7	8	9	10	11	12	13

N	O	P	Q	R	S	T	U	V	W	X	Y	Z
14	15	16	17	18	19	20	21	22	23	24	25	26

John was the __ __ __ __ __ __ in Ephesus
        16 1 19 20 15 18

John loved __ __ __ __ __ __ __ with and
          23 1 12 11 9 14 7

__ __ __ __ __ __ __ __ from Jesus
12 5 1 18 14 9 14 7

Jesus lived a __ __ __ __ __ __ __ life
              16 5 18 6 5 3 20

When You accept Jesus' gift of salvation, the __ __ __ __
                                               8 15 12 25

__ __ __ __ __ __ comes to live in me
19 16 9 18 9 20

Don't Believe Everything You Hear

```
M X E K Y I X V B P V S Z F K
T G W T E A C H I N G S T J W
C O N F U S I O N Y I C R U J
U O F J H L O N T V W N U N F
Y Z W Q X B D P P M R I T G A
R C N I D I K K G B O T H R L
U D C M S Y W E V S T V V I S
U I Q A T D T P T S F A F F E
P R A D R F O X N W Z H K F W
A W P L K E V M S Y P G F X W
F W I D B W F F A W R N Y A V
B P M Y U T B U F D D E P L R
O J L L W X Z C L Z Q W K Z D
W G S T O X B A N I S H E D C
V W L F A I T H C L S W J K R
```

BANISHED	CAREFUL	CONFUSION
FAITH	FALSE	NEW
TEACHINGS	TRUTH	WISDOM

Dear God,

Your Friend,

Week 8

Learning from the Good, the Bad, and the Ugly

Leader/Parent Overview

Key Points

- Our behavior matters. We learn valuable lessons from three men.
- Gaius was a good guy. He is someone who encourages others.
- Diotrephes is a bad man. He is a bully and treats people with meanness. Talk about how this type of behavior isn't acceptable. When you see someone bullied you need to speak up.
- We don't know much about Demetrius. John felt the need to put him in the letter and say how he's been hearing great things about him. This tells us that others watch us and how we behave. Even when we think no one is watching, we had better be on good behavior.

Additional Questions

- Do you watch how others behave? What have you learned from them?
- Why is it important to stand up for people who are bullied?
- Have you had any experiences with bullies?
- If someone were watching you, what do you think they would know about you through your behavior?

Learning From The Good, The Bad, and The Ugly

Hello Friend!

This is John one last time. As you remember, I am the Pastor of the church in Ephesus. As a Pastor, it is my job to know the people in my church. There are three people in my church that stand out. Two of them for good reasons. One of them for bad reasons. No matter if it is for good or bad we can learn lessons from them.

First up is Gaius. He is a man who encourages others. If someone is lonely or sad he wants to cheer them up. He loves to serve. He serves God by walking out His two best rules. He loves God with all of him and he loves others. He shows God's love to other Christians and to those he doesn't even know.

Our next person is one who is here for all the wrong reasons. His name is Diotrephes. He is a bully. Whenever I, John, can come back to Ephesus, I will talk with him about his actions. He talks about people behind their backs, spreads lies, and much more. These actions make God sad. He is not behaving well. He is not a good example to people who don't believe.

Last we have Demetrius. I have heard from some of you in my church about Demetrius. Each of you have been speaking well of him. He is doing good in living a God-centered life. Well done!

Do you see how I have put the two good at the top and bottom? This way we can start and end with good reports!

One day soon I hope to come back. There are so many more things I want to share with you. Until then, I will continue to write letters.

Taking a Deeper Look

1. What are God's two best rules?

_____
_____
_____
_____
_____

2. Over these last few weeks how have you been doing on walking out God's two best rules?

_____
_____
_____
_____
_____

3. Out of the three people John wrote about, which one teaches you the best lesson? Why?

_____
_____
_____
_____
_____

Seeing Z.O.E. Reflected in this Passage

Z - Gaius showed he was *Zealous* to follow God's two best rules. He showed his love for God to everyone, even strangers. Do you know that you can do simple things to show God's love. You can hold a door open, smile, or simply say hello. What is something you will do?

_____
_____
_____
_____
_____

O - Diotrephes was a very *Disobedient* man. His *Disobedience* impacted people around him. Have you been around a *Disobedient* person? Did what he or she did impact you? How does being around an *Obedient* person impact you?

_____
_____
_____
_____
_____

E - As a Christian you can *Expect* that someone is watching the way you act. You may or may not know that they are! This means we should always be letting God's light shine through us. Do you let God's light shine whenever you go out? How about at home?

_____
_____
_____
_____
_____

Memory Verse

"But as he who called you is holy, you also be holy in all your conduct."
1 Peter 1:15

What are some actions that show good behavior? How often do you do these? What are some actions that you need help with?

_____
_____
_____
_____
_____
_____

Being Z.O.E.

For this last challenge we are going to look at everything we have learned through John's letters. What was the best truth you learned?

_____
_____
_____
_____
_____

How are you applying this to your life?

_____
_____
_____
_____
_____

Have you shared this truth with your friends or family? If not, pick someone this week to share it with. Tell them why it means so much to you.

_____
_____
_____
_____
_____

The Good, The Bad, and The Ugly

The Good, The Bad, and The Ugly

Directions: Match the numbers to the letters to reveal the answer

A	B	C	D	E	F	G	H	I	J	K	L	M
1	2	3	4	5	6	7	8	9	10	11	12	13

N	O	P	Q	R	S	T	U	V	W	X	Y	Z
14	15	16	17	18	19	20	21	22	23	24	25	26

John wrote __ __ __ __ __ letters and
          20 8 18 5 5

one __ __ __ __ __ __
    7 15 19 16 5 12

Gaius __ __ __ __ __ __ __ __ __ __ others. This
       5 14 3 15 21 18 1 7 5 4

means he cheered them up and made God __ __ __ __ __
                                       8 1 16 16 25

Diotrephes was a __ __ __ __ __. His actions made God
                  2 21 12 12 25

__ __ __. He is an example of how we shouldn't act.
19 1 4

Demetrius lived a __ __ __ - __ __ __ __ __ __
                   7 15 4   3 5 14 20 5 18

__ __ life. This means he loved God with __ __ __ of him!
5 4   1 12 12

The Good, The Bad, and The Ugly

```
D F Y K C O H O Z Q T A G G T
B S D T U D I R D P L E F O J
P E H J P Q T G U X E Y E W M
F C H U R C H G Z U S O N V P
C R C A N H I V D S S P C W A
J G H Q V T W L M E O G O N S
G X E X O I R R K R N F U M T
W P E K T L O H X N S B R D O
M B R X Y D Q R Y C U W A R R
N D U Z K N R L G L N J G P R
W G P C N X Y M T N T T E R D
X S K P H L O N E L Y S X K H
I H Y L Q P S G S E R V E T I
A C T I O N S X N C Y D E Q C
Z G X V G N G F T R F E T Q Z
```

ACTIONS	BEHAVIOR	CHEERUP
CHURCH	ENCOURAGE	LESSONS
LONELY	PASTOR	SERVE

Dear God,

Your Friend,

Acknowledgements

Above all, I thank God, my Creator, the One who formed me for His purpose. Without Him, my life would be meaningless. I am ever so grateful for the gifts He has given me. To Him be all the glory, praise, and honor.

To my family: John and Fay, Jonathan and Shannon, Uncle Richard, Clayton, and Brickman. You are my rocks, my support, inspirations, the ones whom I can count on. I'm so blessed that God gave me you. Love you all.

To Darin and Debbie: Debbie, thank you for giving me the superhero name ZoeWoman so many years ago. Darin, thank you for designing the covers and the coloring pages. You made it all come to life with your artwork.

To Ruthie and Vi: Even though we are generations apart we are kindred spirits. I hope that in my senior years, I can be as wise as you are in the Bible. You reflect our Lord and Savior in every circumstance. You are amazing witnesses.

To Robert: Thank you for partnering with me in publishing. I thank you for your support, advice, and help throughout this process.

To Jan, Valerie, and Victoria: Thank you for being my eyes through the editing process. Ladies, you are a blessing in my life.

www.ingramcontent.com/pod-product-compliance
Lightning Source LLC
LaVergne TN
LVHW081355060426
835510LV00013B/1833